T0146637

Eradicating Cyber Bullying:
Through Online Training, Reporting & Tracking System

Ronald W. Holmes, Ph.D.

Publisher, The Holmes Education Post, LLC

"An Education Focused Internet Newspaper"

authorHOUSE®

AuthorHouse™
1663 Liberty Drive
Bloomington, IN 47403
www.authorhouse.com
Phone: 1 (800) 839-8640

Published by AuthorHouse 08/10/2017

ISBN: 978-1-5462-0306-3 (sc)
ISBN: 978-1-5462-0304-9 (hc)
ISBN: 978-1-5462-0305-6 (e)

Library of Congress Control Number: 2017911992

Print information available on the last page.

Table of Contents

ACKNOWLEDGEMENT

Just as face-to-face bullying is prevalent with students in K-20 educational institutions and adults in the workplace, cyber bullying is prevalent with students and adults respectively in the same environments. In writing this book, "Eradicating Cyber Bullying through Online Training, Reporting and Tracking System," I was concerned about the number of students who are cyber bullied in various educational settings, organizations and communities.

Within the past three years, I wrote a book on both "How to Eradicate Hazing;" "How to Eradicate Schoolyard Bullying;" and "How to Eradicate Workplace Bullying." The hazing book focused on middle school, high school and college students; the schoolyard bullying book focused on elementary, middle and high school students; and the workplace bullying book focused on employees in various organizations. Also, each book is equipped with an online program organized in a distance learning format.

Cyber bullying is a serious and dangerous act, so educational institutions, businesses, government agencies and healthcare must engage in research-based solutions to protect the safety, health and livelihood of their students and employees. These solutions must incorporate anti-bullying policies and procedures earmarked to address cyber bullying and prohibit discrimination and harassment against all people including those in protected groups such as race, color, national origin, sex, disability and religion.

Considering the time, energy and commitment it takes to write a book, I would like to thank my wife, Constance C. Holmes, for being the editor for the book. Her continued dedication and unwavering support to my work and service to public education is greatly appreciated. She truly understands the importance of education and my supreme sacrifice to this calling.

DEDICATION

This book is dedicated to all the innocent victims of bullying particularly students who are confronted with cyber bullying in educational settings and communities, lost their mental health or livelihood due to cyber bullying and other forms of violence in these environments.

It is my hope that this book will serve as a vehicle to improve educational institutions' policies and procedures for their students and contribute to the eradication of cyber bullying in the U.S. and abroad.

FOREWORD

Cyber bullying is bullying through technology such as the mobile telephone and Internet to psychologically harm the victim. Traditional bullying such as schoolyard or workplace respectively can occur through verbal abuse, physical abuse or withdrawal of information from employees to prohibit them from performing their jobs. (Sarkar 2015). When the abuse is through electronic devices, this also relates to cyber bullying.

In this millennium, cyber-bullying and traditional bullying are causing an alarming number of students and employees to be confronted by their bullies or perpetrators in the school, home, community or workplace. Some of these perpetrators in the workplace are considered the same perpetrators from the schoolyard as suggested in numerous studies.

As such, students and employees are facing a high level of depression and anxiety when they are bullied in these organizations, as well as when they witness their peers or colleagues being bullied. In the schoolyard, for example, bullies are causing 1.2 million students to drop out of school annually (National Education Association). In the workplace, 65.6 million working Americans experienced or witnessed abusive conduct during their workday (Curry, 2016).

Therefore, it is imperative that organizations such as educational institutions, businesses and government agencies learn proactive ways to address traditional bullying and cyber bullying.

Traditional bullying and cyber bullying lead to stress in those who are bullied, as well as witness the bullying. Bullying can lead to a negative image of organizations and make it difficult to hire talented workers. Traditional bullying and cyber bullying also lead to litigation and added cost to organizations. In fact, the damage inflicted by cyber-bullying can potentially be greater than traditional bullying. The reason is that the bully and bystanders may be anonymous and may not know the level of pain inflicted on the victim and may extend the level of pain inflicted on the victim. In traditional bullying, the bully and bystanders know the level of pain inflicted on the victim and may reduce the level depending on how the victim is affected by it (Sarkar, 2015).

Thus, whether it is traditional bullying or cyber-bullying, it is time to eradicate bullying in order to protect the safety, health and livelihood of individuals. This book provides research-based solutions on "what to do" to eradicate cyber bullying in the school, home, community and workplace through the resource of an Online National Anti-Cyber Bullying Curriculum and Web Based Reporting, Tracking, Training and Documentation System (Tell24-7.com).

What is Cyber Bullying?

Cyber bullying is a dangerous and serious act in various organizations with many students and employees experiencing psychological effects such as stress and depression from it. So, the critical question to be asked is: What is Cyber bullying?

What is Cyber bullying?

First, it is important to understand that "bullying is when a student is exposed, repeatedly and over time to negative actions on the part of one or more students and he or she has difficulty defending himself and herself" (Olweus cited in Wood, 2013). Bullying might come in the form of direct bullying such as verbal or physical aggression and indirect or relational bullying such as cyber bullying or sexting. Verbal aggression might include teasing, taunting, name calling, making threats and spreading rumors. Physical aggression might include assaulting, kicking, hitting and destroying physical property. Relational aggression might include staring deliberately at someone, using threatening or offensive gestures towards the person and leaving hurtful messages on electronic devices.

Cyber bullying is when an individual is tormented, threatened, harassed, humiliated, embarrassed or otherwise targeted by another individual using the Internet, interactive and digital technologies or mobile phones. Sexting is sending sexually explicit photos, videos or messages electronically from the cell phone. In the workplace, cyber bullying and sexting are equally as pervasive as verbal and physical aggressions.

Cyber bullying may occur in different forms such as hacking a person's account, sending intimidating or threatening emails and posting derogatory comments on a person's social networking site.

When these negative comments are posted on the social networking site of the victim, simultaneously, the victim's friends, colleagues, family members and others may become aware it (Sarka, 2015).

Thus, the negative impact of cyber bullying can potentially be greater than traditional bullying. When the bully and bystanders inflict pain on the victim, they equally get affected in traditional bullying. In cyber bullying, however, the bully and bystanders may be anonymous and may not know the level of pain inflicted on the victim and may extend the level of pain inflicted on the victim (Sarkar, 2015).

While there are 49 states with anti-bullying laws (See Figure 1) and several states with cyber bullying laws and criminal sanctions, it is important that stakeholders such as parents and teachers recognize the signs of a child being bullied or being a bully respectively such as being afraid to go to school and becoming increasingly frustrated in school (Bullying Statistics, 2013). Other examples might include the victim's grades declining and the perpetrator's constantly referred to the school administrator for discipline (SBG).

Figure 1
Anti-Bullying Laws in U.S. States and Enactment Date

Georgia 1999	Virginia 2005	Utah 2008
New Hampshire 2000	Texas 2005	Florida 2008
Colorado 2001	Tennessee 2005	North Carolina 2009
Louisiana 2001	Maine 2005	Wyoming 2009
Mississippi 2001	Nevada 2005	Alabama 2009
Oregon 2001	Idaho 2006	Massachusetts 2010
West Virginia 2001	South Carolina 2006	Wisconsin 2010
Connecticut 2002	Alaska 2006	New York 2010
New Jersey 2002	New Mexico 2006	Missouri 2010
Oklahoma 2002	Delaware 2007	North Dakota 2011
Washington 2002	Iowa 2007	Hawaii 2011
Arkansas 2003	Illinois 2007	Michigan 2011
California 2003	Kansas 2007	South Dakota 2012
Rhode Island 2003	Minnesota 2007	
Vermont 2004	Ohio 2007	
Arizona 2005	Pennsylvania 2007	
Indiana 2005	Nebraska 2008	
Maryland 2005	Kentucky 2008	

State with No Anti-Bullying Law   *As of 2017*
Montana

States with Cyber Bullying laws and Criminal Sanctions
Arkansas, Missouri, Nevada, North Carolina, Tennessee and Washington

Similar to bullying, there are 44 states with anti-hazing laws (See Figure 2). Hazing comprises of "any activity expected of someone joining a group that humiliates, degrades, abuses or endangers regardless of the person's willingness to participate" in the activity. The activity is normally affiliated with an individual being physically and psychologically abused, depriving of sleep, carrying unwarranted objects, consuming alcohol, participating in sexual acts and paddling (Nuwer cited in Chang 2011). Hazing activity can occur on or off campus of educational institutions, by an individual alone or acting with others for the purpose of pledging, being initiated into, affiliating with holding office in an organization or maintaining membership in an organization.

Figure 2
Anti-Hazing Laws in U.S. States

State / Enactment Date		
Illinois 1901	Pennsylvania 1986	Tennessee 1995
Rhode Island 1909	Missouri 1987	Texas 1995
North Carolina 1913	South Carolina 1987	West Virginia 1995
Louisiana 1920	Connecticut 1988	Minnesota 1997
Michigan 1931	Georgia 1988	Colorado 1999
Virginia 1975	Iowa 1989	Nevada 1999
California 1976	Maine 1989	Vermont 1999
Indiana 1976	Utah 1989	Arizona 2001
New Jersey 1980	Mississippi 1990	Florida 2002
Alabama 1981	Oklahoma 1990	Maryland 2002
Ohio 1982	Idaho 1991	
Arkansas 1983	Delaware 1992	
New York 1983	New Hampshire 1993	
Oregon 1983	Washington (State) 1993	
Wisconsin 1983	Nebraska 1994	
Massachusetts 1985	North Dakota 1995	
Kansas 1986		
Kentucky 1986		

State with No Anti-Hazing Law   *As of 2017*
Alaska
Hawaii
Montana
New Mexico
South Dakota
Wyoming

Whether it is traditional bullying, cyber bullying or hazing, they all may have the same psychological and physical effect on individuals such as stress, illness and death. Organizations such as educational institutions are confronted with these dangerous acts committed by perpetrators throughout the U.S. and abroad. They must employ research-based interventions to eradicate traditional bullying, cyber bullying and hazing associated with these institutions.

As a result, this book discusses research-based strategies on "what to do" to eradicate cyber bullying in the school, home, community and workplace through the resource of an Online National Anti-Cyber Bullying Curriculum and Web Based Reporting, Tracking, Training and Documentation System (Tell24-7.com).

Types of Cyber bullying

There are seven different types of cyber bullying. They include outing, flaming, denigration, exclusion, cyber-stalking, harassment and impersonation (Siegle found in Herrera, 2014). Outing, for example, "occurs when an individual or group deliberately posts, displays or forwards text or images which are sexual in nature, embarrassing, or contain personal information without the person's consent, thereby revealing some sort of secret." Flaming "occurs when two or more people engage in a brief, heated exchange through any form or media." Denigration is defined as "making derogatory comments about someone and disseminating the information online." Exclusion "is intended to make the victim feel ostracized by deliberately refusing to accept them as an online friend or to communicate with them on a social networking site." Cyper-stalking can include "using technology to stalk another individual through threats, continual harassment, intimidation or behaviors which may otherwise make the victim feel unsafe. Harassment "involves repeatedly sending rude, offensive, or cruel messages" to the victim (Popovic-Citie et al. found in Herrera, 2014). Impersonation "involves pretending to be someone else online" (Wade & Beran found in Herrera, 2014).

According to Strom et al. found in Herrera (2014), a romantic breakup followed by the action of spreading lies and threats on an individual is the number one reason cyber bullying occurs. It is thought that cyber bullying might have a more damaging effect than traditional bullying since ordinary communication is obsolete due to a lack of social presence within online communication. The bully is generally unable to proficiently assess the victim's reaction and vice versa (Mark & Ratliffe found in Herrera, 2014).

In a research study, cyber bullies were asked the reason they participated in cyber bullying; the findings revealed that 72% of respondents noted that they cyber bullied for the support of another peer online; 22% of the respondents noted that they found it to be funny; 17% of the respondents noted that they felt it would not cause any problem or harm to anyone; and 17% of the respondents noted that they did not know why they participated in cyber bullying or they just did it to belong with others (Ratliffe found in Herrera, 2014).

Real-Life Stories of Cyber bullying

Cyber bullying is the new form of bullying. In 2015, 24% of students in middle school and 15.5% of students in high school were cyber bullied according to the Center for Disease Control. In a recent study by the Pew Research Center, 41% of U.S. adults have been subjected to cyber bullying (Sander, R, 2017). While there are seven different types of cyber bullying, the following provides stories of individuals who have been victimized of cyber bullying in each of the types.

Outing – "occurs when an individual or group deliberately posts, displays or forwards text or images which are embarrassing, or contain personal information without the person's consent."

The individual is a new president of a college that never had a female administrator in charge of the institution. To the perpetrators' disapproval of the appointment, the individual receives acts of cyber bullying such as the perpetrators taking a photo of her without permission at a time when she is frowning or not looking her best to take a picture. Subsequently, the perpetrators spread the image over the Internet for other employees to see the photo and make fun of the president. According to the Pew Research Center, purposeful embarrassment is considered one of the most common forms of harassment.

Flaming-"occurs when two or more people engage in a brief, heated exchange through any form or media."

The individual is a department chair for a public college. When she attempted to implement changes in her department to improve services at the college, the employees complained to the union.

The union representative sided with the employees and engaged in heated exchange of negative comments about the department chair through the college's email system and newspaper. The employees joined in the dispute via newspaper making it very difficult for the department chair to do her job.

Denigration-is defined as "making derogatory comments about someone and disseminating the information online."

The individual is an administrator of a private school system whose experience was all in a public school system. Because the students, parents and graduates of the private school system did not accept the individual's appointment, they collectively posted derogatory comments about the individual on Facebook and Instagram.

Exclusion—"is intended to make the victims feel ostracized by deliberately refusing to accept them as an online friend or to communicate with them on a social networking site."

A teenage student was forced to complete high school through home school as result of being cyber bullied by classmates. The perpetrators created an inflammatory webpage making fun of the student. They accused the student of being a pedophile and enlisted the social networking community to participate in the harassment of the student (Lightburn, 2090). According to the Pew Research Center, offensive-name calling is considered one of the most common forms of harassment.

Cyber-stalking-can include "using technology to stalk another individual through threats, continual harassment, intimidation or behaviors which may otherwise make the victim feel unsafe.

A high school student was repeatedly stalked on her MySpace account with threats of bodily harm. Parents reported the incidents to the school system as a means to stop the perpetrators. When the cyber bullying became too severe for the student to handle, she took her own life. (PureSight)

Harassment-"involves repeatedly sending rude, offensive, or cruel messages" to the victim.

A high school student was repeatedly harassed once he shared his secret that he was gay. Before committing suicide, the perpetrators not only harassed him online with cruel messages but they also via telephone and face-to-face. (PureSight)

Impersonation-"involves pretending to be someone else online,"

A middle school student constantly received cruel messages on her MySpace account from a former boyfriend. The perpetrator used a false identity to disguise himself. As the cyber bullying became too harsh for the victim to handle, she took her own life (Lightburn, 2009).

Types of Social Networking Sites & Use by Teens

While there are seven different types of cyber bullying, perpetrators bully victims such as teens on various social networking sites. The following provides information on the five most used social media sites by teens. They include Facebook, Instagram, Snapchat, Twitter and Google (Pew Research Center, 2015),

Facebook®—As of June 2017, there were 2 billion Facebook users. In the U.S., approximately 71% of all teens ages 13-17 report using Facebook (Pew Research, 2015). Users of Facebook such as teens are able to connect with their friends, family members and individuals who share the same interests. They can exchange messages, post digital photos, share digital videos and links. They can also use various software apps and receive notifications when their friends update their profiles or create new posts (Wikipedia).

Instagram®—As of April 2017, there were 700 million Instagram users (Wikipedia). In the U.S., approximately 52% of all teens ages 13-17 report using Instagram (Pew Research Center, 2015). Through a mobile app, Instagram allows users such as teens to edit and upload photos and videos; and share the postings with others publicly or privately. Users "can add hashtags to their posts, link the post to other content on Instagram, connect their Instagram account to other social media profiles such as Facebook and Twitter and share photos to those profiles as well" (Wikipedia).

Snapchat®-As of May 2016, there were 10 million Snapchat daily users (Wikipedia). In the U.S., approximately 41% of all teens ages 13-17 report using Snapchat (Pew Research Center, 2015). Snapchat allows users such as teens to post pictures and messages online for a short period of time before they become inaccessible (Wikipedia). A number of teens share private and important information with selected friends. They also use snapshot to take selfies and express how they feel (Lohmann, 2016).

Twitter®-As of 2016, there are more than 319 million users of Twitter. In the U.S. approximately 33% of all teens ages 13-17 report using Twitter (Pew Research Center, 2015). Twitter allows users to post and send messages or tweets to their following using 140 characters or less (Wikipedia).

Google+®-As of 2013, there were 540 million active users of Google+ (Wikipedia). In the U.S., approximately 33% of all teens ages 13-17 report using Google (Pew Research Center, 2015). Google+ a social networking platform, allows users such as teens to post photos and engage in ongoing communication with friends, family members etc. on different topics of concern. Users can also group their relationships with other acquaintances in a circle (Lohmann, 2016)

According to a study by the Pew Research Center, African American teens report using the Internet more frequently than other teens (Hispanic 34% and White 19%). Also, teens from low socio-economic families report using Facebook more frequently than any other social networking platforms; whereas, teens from high socio-economic families report using Snapshot and Twitter more frequently than any other platforms.

Additionally, the average teen has 201 Facebook friends; 37% of teens send messages to friends every day; 86% of teens comment on a friend's wall; 83% comment on friends' pictures; 66% send private messages to friends; 58% send text messages using the site; 52% send group messages; 55% of teens have given their personal information to someone they don't know, including photos and physical descriptions; 29% of teens have posted mean information, embarrassing photos or spread rumors about someone; 29% have been stalked or contacted by a stranger or someone they don t know; 24% have had private or embarrassing information made public without their permission and 22% have been cyberpranked" (ToTenReviews).

STATISTICS – Traditional Bullying & Cyber Bullying

As reported by the American Society for the Positive Care of Children (ASPCC), 28% of American students in grades 6-12 experienced bullying; and 20% of American students in grades 9-12 experienced bullying. Approximately, 30% of teens admit to bullying others.

As a witness to bullying, 70.6% of teens say they have seen bullying in their schools; and 70.4% of staff members at school have seen bullying too. Bullying ends within 10 seconds (approximately 57% of the time) when bystanders intervene.

Additionally, ASPCC reported that 6% of 6th–12th graders experienced cyber bullying; 16% of 9th – 12th grades experienced cyber bullying the past year and 52.2% of LGBT experienced cyber bullying as well.

In 2015, 24% of students in middle school and 15.5% of students in high school were cyber bullied according to the Center for Disease Control.

These statistics show the seriousness and pervasiveness of traditional bullying and cyber bullying in the school culture and community.

Bullying Perspectives

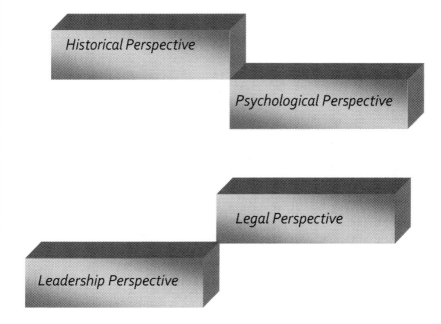

With traditional bullying and cyber bullying being interwoven in society and constantly occurring in the community, schools and workplace, we must clearly understand the meaning of bullying from a historical, psychological, legal, and leadership perspective.

Historical Perspective

In this century, bullying has increasingly become a major societal problem as reported in the media. It may come in the form of direct bullying such as verbal or physical aggressions and indirect bullying or relational aggression such as cyber bullying or sexting. In 1999, the Columbine High School massacre in Colorado brought attention to this epidemic. At that time, it was perhaps one of the most deadly school shootings in America where two students killed twelve classmates, a teacher and wounded twenty-four others before killing themselves. Over a year, these students strategically planned their retaliation against their schoolmates who had bullied them (Raywid cited in Fegenbush 2010).

Prior to this incident in the U.S., little or no research was done about bullying except in countries such as Australia and Europe. In the 1970s, Dan Olweus considered the founding father of bullying, published a book called the Aggression in the Schools: Bullies and Whipping Boys in 1973 in Scandinavia and in 1978 in the U.S. After a 1983 suicide-related death of three adolescent boys severely bullied by their perpetrators in Norway, Norwegian officials initiated a national campaign against bullying in schools. With a basis for understanding this bullying phenomenon, Olweus' research caught on in other countries in the 1980s and 1990s, and a plethora of research on bullying was studied by American researchers near 2001 (Fegenbush, 2010).

In 2001, for instance, a national study was conducted in the U.S. of 15,686 sixth through tenth graders about bullying. Approximately 29.9% of the students reported moderate to frequent involvement in bullying, 13% identified themselves as bullies, 10.6% identified themselves as victims and 6.3% identified themselves as bully-victims according to Espelage & Swearer (cited in Wood 2013).

In 2010, the Josephson Institute of Ethics conducted a large study in the U.S. regarding the attitudes of 43,321 high schools students. From this study, 50% of the students admitted they had bullied a person in the previous year, and 47% indicated they were bullied, taunted or teased in a way that frustrated them in the previous year (Josephson Institute of Ethics cited in Wood 2013).

Just as bullying is prevalent on the schoolyard, it is also prevalent in the workplace. In some countries such as Australia, workplace bullying is illegal. In the U.S., workforce bullying is not illegal. Workplace bullying was introduced through Carroll Brodsky's 1976 book (The Harassed Worker). Brodsky defined "harassment behavior as repeated and persistent attempts by an individual to torment, wear down, frustrate, or elicit a reaction from another individual. Brodsky documented that bullying provided strong effects on a victim's health and well-being. Brodsky also described victims of bullying as conscientious employees who were typically overachievers in the workplace" (Brodsky cited in Bame, 2013).

In the late 1980s, adult bullying was researched by Heinze Leymann and associated with mobbing. Namie & Namie compared mobbing "to, the animal behavior of smaller animals in packs attacking single larger animals. Leymann compared mobbing as a recurring hostile and unethical communication in the workplace by one or more individuals aimed toward a defenseless individual over a period of six months or longer." While the U.S. adopted the bullying term, other countries adopted the mobbing term during the 1990s. As the bullying phenomenon continued to rise in the U.S. and abroad, the International Labor Office reported that the global cost to bullying to exceed millions of dollars in losses from sick leave, absenteeism, and medical expenses (Bame, 2013).

Due to the pervasiveness of this epidemic throughout Australia, for instance, the Workplace Health and Safety Department of Industrial Relations in 2002 published a report of common behaviors of workplace bullies in organizations. Some of these behaviors include verbal and physical abuse, undermining of work, deliberate, planned activity to discredit, fabricating complaints, and overloading of work on employees. Other common bullying behaviors include blocking an employee's advancement or promotion on the job, assigning excessive work and criticizing an employee unjustifiably (Bame, 2013).

While traditional bullying such as schoolyard and workplace are prevalent in society, the damage inflicted by cyber bullying can potentially be greater than traditional bullying (Sarkar, 2015). Through cyber bullying, ordinary communication is distorted due to a lack of social presence within online communication. The bully is generally unable to proficiently assess the victim's reaction and vice versa (Mark & Ratliffe found in Herrera, 2014). The bully might convey messages he or she normally would not convey in face-to-face communication.

Cyber bullying emerged from the advancements of technology and devices. Similar to traditional bullying, it involves the perpetrator and victim. It also involves a third party, the bystander. Through cyber bullying, individuals can engage in inappropriate use of technology such as taking video clips or photos of other individuals in various settings (school, home, community or workplace). Without consent, the victims of the posting can find their images on popular sites such as Instagram, Facebook, Youtube and Twitter. As such, this enables cyber bullying to expand more frequently than traditional bullying and potentially pose a greater impact on the victims.

Psychological Perspective

At the pinnacle, bullying is a dangerous act and associated to a third degree burn with the potential of leaving a deep and permanent damage or scarring to the victims. Some psychological effects of bullying are stress, depression, alcohol abuse, mental health and even suicide. These effects not only impact the victims of bullying, but also the witnesses to bullying.

Whether it is traditional bullying or cyber bullying, bullying is a complex phenomenon. At the schoolyard level, researchers such as Swearer and Espelager advocate that intervention programs on bullying will be most effective if the programs target multiple environments such as the home, community and school (Swearer & Espelage cited in Wood, 2013). The rationale is that bullying does not occur in isolation since the relationships across family, peer, school, and community contexts will impact the engagement or non-engagement in bullying and victimization behaviors. See Figure 3 of Swearer & Espelage's Social-ecological framework among youth.

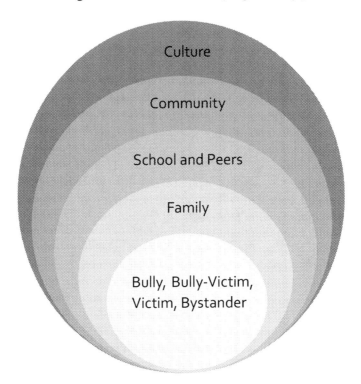

Figure 3

A Social-ecological framework of bullying among youth.

Culture

Community

School and Peers

Family

Bully, Bully-Victim, Victim, Bystander

At the workplace level, researchers such as Pearson and Porath advocate that an "integrated approach including individual, organizational and societal levels is required to tackle workplace mistreatment" (Pearson & Porath cited in Hodgins et al., 2014). The rationale is that employees who experience workplace bullying are disenchanted by the lack of response by the organization, as well as the organization's unwillingness or inability to create relevant interventions to proactively prevent bullying.

Bullying, particularly in the form of cyber bullying, "potentially threatens several basic human needs." They include self-esteem, belonging and control (Williams, Cheung, & Choi found in Lightburn, 2009). The following is an excerpt of the these basic human needs related to cyber bullying according to Lightburn (2009).

Control

As a person is unaware of the identity of the bully and the reason for being harassed, cyber bullying threatens a person's perceived sense of control. Since the person or victim is unable to interact with the perpetrator, the sense of control is lost. This was the case of 13-year-old Megan Meier who reportedly received cruel MySpace messages from a former boyfriend who used a fictitious identity. It will be discussed with other cases in a proceeding chapter.

Belonging

In this millennium, a great number of individuals use electronic devices such as the Internet for social connection. When a person is ostracized through cyber bullying, this can deprive a person or victim of his or her sense of belonging to a particular social connection such as a school or community. This was the case in an Ontario teen, David Knight which will be discussed in a proceeding chapter. His class mates defamed him on the Internet as being a pedophile. Because of the severity of the harassment, it forced David to lose his sense of belonging to the school community and forced him to complete high school through home school.

Self-Esteem

Cyber bullying can have a deleterious influence on a person's self-esteem. When a person or victim, for example, is repeatedly harassed with negative communication by the perpetrator, this can diminish or minimize the person's sense of self-esteem if he or she internalizes the negative communication as a result of his shortcomings. This was the case in a Canadian teen, Ghyslain Raze which will be discussed in a proceeding chapter. Raze produced a film which gained world-wide attention. Because of humiliation and unflattering attention, Ghyslain lost his self-esteem forcing him into psychiatric care.

In order to understand human development, psychologist Urie Bronfenbrenner proposed in 1979 a theory of ecological-systems. This system is comprised of "five socially organized subsystems that guide human growth and development" through a child's social relationships and surrounding environment. They include microsystem, mesosystem, exosystem, macrosystem and chronosystem. The microsystem relates to the interaction a child has with his immediate environment such as school, home, daycare, work, peers, teachers or family members. For example, a child who has a nourishing home with parents and siblings, attends a safe school with supportive teachers and peers can benefit positively from this type of climate.

The mesosytem comprises of the interactions between the different components of a child's microsystem and on how the environments impacts his or her development. One example would be the relationship between the child's guardian and teacher. For example, a child's parent who attends Parent Teacher Student Association meetings regularly and volunteers in the child's classroom and school activities can have a positive impact on the child's development because the different components of the microsystem are working harmoniously together.

The exosystem consists of environments that do not encompass the child in an active role but still has an impact on him or her. For example, a child's parent who gets a raise or fired from a job can have a deleterious influence on the child although the child did not have anything to do with the employer's decision.

The macrosystem relates to the cultural environments in which a child resides, as well as the influences from all of the systems (microsystem, mesosystem and exosystems) have on the individual. For instance, a child's living in a particular city, state or country can be different from another child and, subsequently, have a positive or negative influence on the individual's development. The chronosystem relates to the changes in the characteristics of a child over time, as well as the environment where the individual resides. For example, a parent's divorce and change in residency from the other spouse can have a negative impact on a child's behavior for a certain period of time.

Thus, a close examination of the ecological systems' theory proposed by psychologist Bronfenbrenner, provides research to help understand why people behave differently in one setting versus another environment such as the home, school, and work (Bronfenbrenner cited in Wood, 2013). School leaders should be knowledgeable of these subsystems that guide human growth and development to improve the learning process.

Legal Perspective

Whether traditional or cyber bullying, bullying is an epidemic in American schools resulting in 49 states to adopt anti-bullying laws. It impacts people of all races, genders, ages, religions and class. When schools are confronted with challenges of students being bullied by their perpetrators, this can lead to potential lawsuits on the basis of Title VI, IX, Section 504 of the Rehabilitation Act of 1973, and Title II of the Americans with Disabilities Act of 1990. Depending on the court cases, schools may be forced to develop, implement and or expand their policies and procedures, as well as take appropriate measures to prevent and respond to bullying incidents.

For effective practices, it is critical that schools appoint an anti-bullying coordinator, train their faculty and staff on anti-bullying preventions, investigate thoroughly bullying incidents and have a communication plan for informing all stakeholders such as parents of anti-bullying prevention activities and the consequences of bullying acts.

Liability issues pertaining to students being bullied or hazed through events such as extra-curricular activities can range from schools being negligent for lack of supervision and failure to provide a reasonable duty of care for the victims. Other liability issues can include failure of schools to provide a safe environment, failure to report an incident to the authority (knowingly or unknowingly), failure to educate, supervise and evaluate school stakeholders (students, faculty members, etc.), failure to develop and implement policies and procedures and failure to properly enforce anti-bullying laws.

While there are no perfect educational institutions, it is essential that schools take proactive steps to effectively address bullying in their settings. Courts are bombarded with legal cases and decisions to determine if there were a "duty of care" between student victims of bullying and educational institutions, as well as if the institutions are "deliberately indifferent" to the harassment that is so severe, pervasive, and objectively offensive that it effectively inhibits the student victims' access to an educational benefit or opportunity. This was the case in the Zeno v. Plains Central School District. The court upheld the decision to grant the student an award of $ 1 million due to school district being in violation of Title VI of the Civil Rights Act of 1964.

Therefore, schools must employ appropriate measures to prevent and respond to bullying incidents (traditional or cyber bullying) on their campuses including students participating in school sponsored activities, students riding school provided transportation and students using school-owned technology. Schools must also employ appropriate measures to prevent and respond to cyber bullying incidents off their campuses of students using their own technology such as MySpace, Facebook,

Instagram or mobile phones. When the incidents are disruptive to the educational environment and violates the victims' rights, the schools should employ appropriate disciplinary action. For understanding of why schools must use appropriate measures to prevent and respond to bullying incidents, Figure 4 provides some examples of legal cases on bullying (cyber and traditional bullying).

Figure 4
Legal Cases

In the 2011 Kara Kowalski v. Berkeley County Schools, et al. cyber-bullying case, a student was suspended for developing a hate website against another student at school which violated the school's harassment, bullying and intimidation (HIB) policy. The Fourth Circuit Court determined that the student's speech exhibited substantial disruption at the school and did not violate the student's First Amendment free speech rights.

In the 2002 J.S. v. Bethlehem Area School District case, The Supreme Court of Pennsylvania upheld the expulsion of a student and the decision of the lower courts that the school district could discipline student for inflammatory and allegedly threatening remarks placed on a website about a school teacher despite the student developed the website off-campus. According to the Supreme Court, there was a "sufficient nexus between the website and the boy school campus to consider the speech as occurring on-campus" (Wikipedia).

In the 2000 Emmett v. Kent School District case, the school district expelled a student for creating a webpage on the Internet at home that provided mock obituaries of students and an online component for visitors on the webpage to vote and determine who would be the next to die or subject of the next mock obituary. The student provided a disclaimer warning students that the webpage was for entertainment and not the property of the school. Since the school district could not provide substantial evidence that the webpage intended or actually threatened anyone, the U.S. District Court for the Western District of Washington, ruled in favor of the student, eliminating all discipline matters from his record.

In the 2012 Zeno v. Pine Plains Central School District case, a high school student was repeatedly harassed and threatened over a number of years based on his race. While the school initially took some disciplinary action against the perpetrators, the bullying continued. The United States District Court for the Southern District of New York upheld the decision of the jury that the school district's action was insufficient or deliberately indifferent to continued harassment of the student. The court also upheld the decision to grant the student an award of $ 1 million due to the school district being in violation of Title VI of the Civil Rights Act of 1964.

In the 2007, L.W. v. Tom River Regional Board of Education case, the New Jersey Supreme Court established that a school district can be held liable when the district fails to act reasonably to end a student-on student harassment complaint on the basis of sexual orientation that creates a hostile educational environment under the Law Against Discrimination for student-on-student harassment.

In the 2011 T.K. and S.K. v. New York City Department of Education case, the federal district court applied a broad standard of liability to the New York public schools, that a female student with disability had stated a valid claim of being denied a free appropriate public education under the federal Individuals with Disabilities Education Act, as result of school officials' failure to remedy student-on-student bullying and harassment based on the victim's disability. Using a 2010 "Dear Colleague Letter " to schools as reference, the federal district court concluded that schools take immediate and appropriate action when responding to bullying incidents that might impede with a special education student's ability to receive an appropriate education.

In the 2011 (Ohio Court of Appeal) Golden v. Milford Exempted Village School District case, involved a sexual aggressor attack on a freshman high school student by several teammates while waiting to be transported on a school-sponsored bus to basketball practice without adult supervision. Once the school district learned of the complaint, it conducted an investigation. Both the parent and student victim filed suit against the basketball coach and school district regarding negligent supervision and civil hazing. The Court of appeal ruled that the acts committed were bullying instead of hazing, and that the basketball coach did not act in a willful manner that would lead to negligence or liability.

In reference to the preceding cases and laws of various federal and state jurisdictions, this should not to be interpreted as giving legal advice regarding the substantive areas of law. The reader should independently consult their legal attorney or legal counselor who has expertise in the case law subject matter discussed in this chapter. While some of the cases might be pending or ongoing, the writer's intent in citing this legal material is for illustration purposes of demonstrating the seriousness of traditional and cyber bullying and the legal, social and monetary effects of not enforcing it.

Leadership Perspective

Effective leaders use data to drive their decision-making regarding the budget, programs, services and performance of employees. Some leaders, for instance, use the concept of zero-based budgeting where each manager's operating budget must be justified from zero for all existing and newly requested programs. This process is conducted each fiscal year compared to budgetary decisions being based on previous year's funding level. For this initiative, data collected is the center of the assessment to analyze the human and financial resources used to determine if there is a need to continue programs or services utilizing these resources (The Holmes Education Post, 2014).

While bullying is an epidemic in society and causing an alarming number of students to commit suicide, school leaders must use data to drive their decision-making regarding the performance of students (academic and discipline). They must have mechanism in place to assess potential bullying incidents and employ appropriate interventions to stop bullying in the schools. As previously discussed, the Zeno v. Pine Plains Central School District case provides an example of the problem schools face when they don't do enough to stop bullying in the learning environment.

School leaders have to become aware of the dangers and seriousness of bullying and provide support to students at the highest level possible. They have to demonstrate or provide their support to students through data driven activities in the learning environment.

In the proceeding chapter, the book highlights information on data-driven initiatives that school leaders can use to drive their decision making regarding the performance of students particularly as it relates to discipline. These initiatives include an Online National Anti-Cyber Bullying Curriculum and a Web Based Reporting, Tracking, Training and Documentation System (Tell24-7.com).

What to do?

Step I-Educate Stakeholders

Bullying is the number one problem in schools according to Kaiser Family Foundation. It is causing students to face a high level of depression and anxiety when they are bullied verbally, physically and electronically. Astoundingly, nearly 160,000 students are absent from school and 1.2 dropout of school annually due to their bullies according to the National Education Association. Additionally, two-third of the students who attempted or completed shootings in America's schools were bullied according to the Secret Service as reported in Behavioral Management.

To ensure the safety of individuals for all "protected classes," (race, ethnicity, gender, religion, disability, nationality and sexual orientation), we must educate all stakeholders such as students, parents, teachers, administrators and community representatives on the policies, procedures and laws for anti-bullying preventions. Students must know clearly what the policies, procedures and laws are regarding bullying in the educational setting. This information must be very transparent regardless of whether students are participating in extra-curricular activities, using school owned technology, attending school sponsored field trips or engaging in other school activities. Students must also know the policies, procedures and laws regarding bullying using their personally owned technology that has a negative impact in the educational setting.

In this millennium, children between ages eight and 18 spend an average of 53 hours a week using electronic media such as Facebook,

Twitter, Myspace, cell phones and video games which leads to lower school grades and students being less happy, according to a study by Kaiser Family Foundation. Through bullying tactics such as sexting and cyberbullying, a third of middle school and high school students have reported being bullied during the school year.

At a Blueprint For Excellence National Conference in Walt Disney World Rosort, Florida, Dr. David Walsh, founder of Mind Positive Parenting indicated that "whatever the brain does a lot is what it gets good at doing." He also indicated that four out of five teens sleep with their cell phones near them, and 20 percent of babies born have some type of technology device. Realizing this, it is essential to teach children in this information age digital awareness to avoid overuse and misuse of technology such as sexting and cyberbullying.

Therefore, anti-bullying prevention information must be an essential part of the Student Code of Conduct and any extra-curricular activity in the academic setting. Along with the faculty sponsor reviewing the policies, procedures and laws with students on bullying for their respective activity, schools must create anti-bullying training including a campus 24-hour anonymous bullying hotline. Students must complete an assessment questionnaire after the training to prove their knowledge and understanding of bullying, as well as know whom to call if they have any concerns. Educational institutions that use a "whole school approach" to address bullying such as the Olweus Bullying Prevention Program, include all stakeholders in the school-wide bullying prevention program.

In addition to completing the assessment questionnaire, students must complete a class assignment such as an essay on bullying which coincides with most states to offer students some type of educational offering on bullying (McCormac, 2015). They must also participate in a school or community service project regarding anti-bullying preventions before participating in a school activity or attending a school sponsored fieldtrip. We have to educate all stakeholders such as students on bullying to ensure that they fully understand the seriousness of the matter. With these requirements intact combined with students maintaining good academic standing and behavior, our expectation for student safety and participation in extra-curricular activities and school sponsored fieldtrips will be enhanced and substantiated by interventions as a viable means to eradicate bullying. Figure 5 provides a sample letter for schools to use to educate student stakeholders, support the Student Code of Conduct and provide proof of anti-bullying prevention compliance.

Jane S. Doe Public School

Office of Administration
3000 Tammy Street East, Lake City, Fla. 32555

Anti-Bullying Prevention Policy Compliance

(Educate Students)

This letter confirms that I have read, fully understand and completed the following requirements of the Jane S. Doe Public School Anti-Bullying Prevention Policy.

Specifically, I have completed the Online Bullying Training, assessment questionnaire and know how to report bullying acts anonymously through the campus 24-hour hotline.

Also, I have completed both a class assignment regarding the anti-bullying training and the required community service project regarding anti-bullying prevention.

Bullying Definition
Bullying is defined as "when a student is exposed, repeatedly and over time, to negative actions on the part of one or more students and he or she has difficulty defending himself or herself."

Florida Cyber Bullying Law
Cyber bullying means "bullying through the use of technology or any electronic communication such as email, Internet, instant messages, faxes, websites and blogs."

Online Cyber Bullying Training
Provides training on the policies, procedures and laws, etc. regarding anti-bullying prevention at Jane S. Doe Public School.

An open door to your future.   *www.janedoepublicschool.com*

Jane S. Doe Public School

Office of Administration
3000 Tammy Street East, Lake City Florida 32555

Anti-Bullying Prevention Policy Compliance

(**Educate Students** – *cont'd*)

Assessment Questionnaire
Provides an assessment of the Online Cyber Bullying Training at Jane S. Doe Public School for reinforcement of anti-bullying prevention.

Campus 24-hour Bullying Hotline
Affords an opportunity for students to report bullying anonymously at Jane S. Doe Public School.

Class Assignment
Provides a class assignment such as an essay to show student proof of understanding anti-bullying prevention before participating in any extra-curricular activities and school sponsored fieldtrips at Jane S. Doe Public School.

Community Service Project
Provides a community service project of student proof of anti-bullying prevention before participating in any extra-curricular activities and school-sponsored fieldtrips at Jane S. Doe Public School.

_____   Office of Administration
Student's Name (Print)

_____   _____
Student's Signature   School Officials' Signature

_____   _____
Date   Date

STEP I – Reinforcement Knowledge Questions

1. How many students are absent from school annually due to their bullies?

2. Why should all school stakeholders such as students and teachers receive training on the policies, procedures and laws on anti-bullying preventions?

3. Why should anti-bullying preventions be an essential part of the Student Code of Conduct and extra-curricular activities?

Step II-Review Policies, Procedures and Laws

Having policies, procedures and laws are very important, but reviewing them are just as important. To eradicate bullying, we must routinely review the policies, procedures and laws on anti-bullying preventions with all stakeholders such as students, faculty members and parents at the school. In Step I of the model, we discussed how to eradicate bullying through the involvement of students. In Step II of the model, we provide examples of how to eradicate bullying through the involvement of parent stakeholders.

Bullying is a major problem for students in America's schools, yet many parents fail to talk to their children about the matter according to Kaiser Family Foundation. Therefore, schools must use social media, newsletters, websites, special events and online bullying training to review and periodically discuss the policies, procedures and laws on anti-bullying preventions. Through social media such as Facebook and Twitter, this will give parents an opportunity to periodically review information on bullying and participate in dialogue for improved knowledge and understanding. Also, through newsletters, websites, special events and online bullying training, this will give parents an opportunity to review pertinent information on bullying and participate in anti-bullying prevention programs in the school setting. Ultimately, this will provide a paper trail of interventions to eradicate bullying from the school culture. Figure 6 provides a sample newsletter to parents illustrating Jane S. Doe Public School's approach to review the policies, procedures and laws of anti-bullying preventions. This same letter can be tailored for faculty, teachers and staff members. Staff members such as bus drivers, food service and security workers, receive the least amount of training on anti-bullying prevention strategies. With inadequate training, this leads to many staff members perceiving bullying differently from students and not sufficiently responding to bullying complaints. Subsequently, this leads to many students being less inclined to report bullying incidents to them (National Education Association, 2010).

Jane S. Doe Public School

Office of Administration
3000 Tammy Street East, Lake City Florida 32555

Anti-Bullying Prevention Policy Compliance
(Review Policies, Procedures and Laws-PPL)

Welcome parents to the 2017 – 2018 academic year! This newsletter focuses on the approaches we are using to promote zero tolerance of bullying at Jane S. Doe Public School (JSDPS).

These strategies include our social media campaign, monthly newsletter, special events and online bullying training:

SOCIAL MEDIA	WEBSITE	ONLINE BULLYING TRAINING
We provide parents an opportunity to follow us on Twitter at Jane S. Doe Public School to gain the latest information on anti-bullying preventions	We have a Bullying Website to display information, review and discuss periodically the policies, procedures and laws on anti-bullying preventions.	We require students to complete the Online Bullying Training at Jane S. Doe Public School before they can participate in any extra-curricular activities and attend any school fieldtrips.
NEWSLETTER	SPECIAL EVENTS	We encourage parents to complete the bullying training to review the policies and laws on anti-bullying preventions.
We will post a monthly newsletter on our website at JSDPS to reiterate the PPL regarding anti-bullying preventions.	We will promote and participate in special events on the campus of Jane S. Doe Public School to review the policies and laws regarding anti-bullying preventions.	We enlist parents to help us reinforce the expectation of anti-bullying preventions to all stakeholders at the school.

Again, we welcome parents to this academic year. Your active involvement is greatly appreciated

An open door to your future.   *www.janedoeuniversity.com*

STEP II – Reinforcement Knowledge Questions

1. What are ways that schools can periodically review and discuss the policies, procedures and laws on anti-bullying preventions?

2. Which school staff receives the least amount of training on anti-bullying prevention strategies?

3. Why are many students less inclined to report bullying incidents to school staff such as bus drivers?

Step III-Address Accountability

People drive their automobiles everyday with the understanding of the laws and consequences for breaking the laws. When they break the laws by speeding, reckless driving or driving under the influence of alcohol, they are held accountable. This might include having to attend a driver's education class, suspension or loss of their driver's license. In the same manner, we must address and ensure that all stakeholders at the school such as teachers are held accountable for the policies, procedures and laws on anti-bullying preventions.

In the previous two steps of the model, we noted the need to educate stakeholders and review policies, procedures and laws about bullying respectively through the involvement of students and parents. In Step III, we provide examples of how to eradicate bullying through the involvement of faculty members such as teachers. For example, schools must use these stakeholders to address accountability through transparency or evidence such as lesson plans, bulletin boards, newsletters, websites, social media and online bullying training.

In addition to faculty members such as teachers receiving anti-bullying training, school officials must require that teachers make sure the policies, procedures and laws on anti-bulling preventions are a part of their course syllabi. For accountability, school officials can assess evidence of this being communicated accordingly through visiting and communicating with teachers in their classrooms, reviewing department chairs' accountability folders and/or posting of syllabi on schools' websites. Just as drivers of automobiles are held accountable for driving safely, teachers must be held accountable for communicating information so the message about anti-bullying prevention is reinforced and taken seriously throughout the educational environment. Figure 7 provides a sample of an abbreviated teacher course syllabus to show or address accountability of bullying through transparency.

Furthermore, school boards must hold school leaders such as administrators accountable for ensuring that they are taking proactive means to address accountability regarding anti-bullying preventions, as well as investigating fully incidents of bullying allegations at the highest level possible. Courts are bombarded with legal cases and decisions to determine if there were a "duty of care" between student victims of bullying and educational institutions, as well as if the institutions are "deliberately indifferent" to the harassment that is so severe, pervasive, and objectively offensive that it effectively inhibits the student victims' access to an educational benefit or opportunity. As previously mentioned, Figure 4 provides examples of some legal cases on bullying.

Jane S. Doe Public School

Office of Administration
3000 Tammy Street East, Lake City Florida 32555

Reading Prep Course Syllabus
Fall 2015

Anti-Bullying Prevention Policy Compliance
(Address Accountability)

Course Description
The purpose of this course is to provide test-taking strategies to prepare students for the reading portion of the state exam.

Course Topics
Reading Comprehension Skills

School Rules & Expectation

Understand that bullying is defined as "when a student is exposed, repeatedly and over time, to negative actions on the part of one or more students and he or she has difficulty defending himself or herself."

Understand that in Florida cyber bullying means "bullying through the use of technology or any electronic communication such as email, Internet, instant messages, faxes, websites and blogs."

I have read, fully understand and agree to Jane S. Doe Public School's anti-bullying prevention policy:

_____   _____
Student's Name (Print)   Student's Signature

                                                          _____
                                                          Date

An open door to your future.   *www.janedoepublicschool.com*

STEP III – Reinforcement Knowledge Questions

1. What are several ways to eradicate bullying through teachers at the school?

2. How can school officials verify that the policies, procedures and laws on anti-bullying preventions are a part of the teachers' course syllabi?

3. Why should school boards hold administrators accountable regarding anti-bullying preventions?

Step IV – Discuss the Characteristics of the Bully, Victim, Bully-victim and Bystander; and the Signs of Bullying

In Step IV, we discuss the characteristics of the bully, victim, bully-victim and bystander. We also discuss the signs of bullying. The bully, for instance, uses power to intimidate or harm a person who is weaker than he or she. The bully appears to be more prevalent in boys than girls and more associated with younger children than older children. The victim is the target of the bullying and receives repeated coercive behavior from the bully. The bully-victim is an individual who bullies others, a victim of the bully and exuberates a high level of depression and aggression. The bystander is the observer or onlooker of the bullying incident and may watch the bullying and not do anything, influence the bullying through gestures and comments or intervene to help the victim from the bully (Wood, 2013).

As previously discussed, there are different types of bullying such as outing and flaming when bullying incidents occur online. Outing "occurs when an individual or group deliberately posts, displays or forwards text or images which are sexual in nature, embarrassing, or contain personal information without the person's consent, thereby revealing some sort of secret. Flaming occurs when two or more people engage in a brief, heated exchange through any form or media."

Thus, it is important that school stakeholders such as parents and teachers recognize the signs of a child being bullied or being a bully. According to Bullying Statistics' website, stakeholders should notice the child presumed as being bullied if the child (1) becomes withdrawn from activities; (2) possesses fear upon going to school; (3) shows increasing symbols of depression; (4) shows a decline in academic achievement; (5) interacts with other children in fear; (6) losses self-confidence in himself or herself; (7) provides evidence of physical scars and (8) losses interest in attending school.

Additionally, Stopbullying.gov provides information on the signs of a child being bullied or being a bully. A number of signs that might reveal a bullying problem if a child has (1) unjustifiable injuries; (2) lost of personal property such as clothes and electronics; (3) constant illnesses such as stomach pain and headaches; (4) severe change in eating habits or lack of eating meals as scheduled; (5) constant nightmares or sleeping difficulties (6) decrease in grades, interest in class assignments or desire to attend school; (7) loss of personal friends and self esteem; (8) seen different in their appearance from their peers and (9) talk about hurting or harming himself/herself physically.

As a child is being a bully to another child, stakeholders such as parents and teachers should notice the bully (1) views violence positively as a viable solution to most problems; (2) shows aggression toward elders and other children; (3) needs to control situations and dominate others; (4) becomes easily upset; (5) shows little sympathy to those who are being bullied or facing issues; and (6) prefers not to help stop bullying, according to research on Bullying Statistics.

Furthermore, a number of signs that might reveal a child is bullying others if the child: (1) becomes involved in verbal and physical fights; (2) has peers who bully other children; (3) becomes more aggressive toward others; (4) gets referred constantly to the administrator's office or assigned school detention; (5) encounters unsubstantiated extra cash or new accessories; (6) accuses others for their own problems; (7) declines to take responsibility for their wrongdoing; (8) worries about their popularity and image and (9) has little or no parental support or has conflicting issues in the home or community.

Schools must become aware of these characteristics of bullying, as well as the signs of bullying. The information (characteristics and signs of bullying) relates directly to Bronfenbrenner's five socially organized subsystems (microsystem, mesosystem, exosystem, macrosystem and chronosystem) that guide human growth and development through a child's social relationships and surrounding environment. The information must become an integral part of schools anti-bullying prevention programs in order to maintain an educational setting that is safe and conducive to learning.

STEP IV – Reinforcement Knowledge Questions

1. What are the four signs of bullying?

2. What are two types of bullying that occur online?

3. How can parents recognize some signs that indicate a child is being bullied or being a bully?

Step V-Implement Activities

It is written that "we learn best by doing." To eradicate bullying from our school, we must implement activities that bring attention to bullying. In the first three steps of the model, we noted the need to educate stakeholders, review policies, procedures and laws and address accountability about bullying respectively through the involvement of faculty members such as teachers. In the fourth step of the model, we discussed the characteristics and signs of bullying. In Step V, we provide examples of how to eradicate bullying through the involvement of school and community organizations.

There are many school-wide bullying prevention programs in the U.S. and abroad designed to stop bullying in schools. One notable program used throughout the World is the Olweus Bullying Prevention Program. As highlighted in Figure 8, the OBPP addresses school bullying with proactive and reactive measures on the school, class and individual levels. According to Fegenbush (2010), Olweus reported the impact of school acts of bullying utilizing the OBPP victim questionnaire of students who had participated in the program for 2.5 years. The survey results of participants pre-and post-tests revealed: (1) a "50% reduction in bullying behaviors; (2) a clear reduction in anti-social behaviors such as vandalism, fighting, and truancy; (3) an increased student satisfaction with school life," etc. This study was replicated in a study called Sheffield Project where students were administered pre-and post-test surveys. The survey results of participants corroborated with those of the OBPP such as, "a 40% reduction rate in student reporting acts of bullying."

As an example of Olweus' proactive measures at the class level, the San Francisco District Attorney George Gascón (DA) coupled with community partners, launched an annual "Bye Bye Bullying" video contest for San Francisco middle and high school students which is the DA's office truancy initiative to keep students in school.

Figure 8

Components of Olweus' Bullying Intervention Program

Level of Implementation	Criteria/Recommendations
Measures at the School Level	Questionnaire Survey School conference day on bully/victim problems Better supervision during recess and lunch time Contact telephone Meeting staff-parents Teacher groups for the development of the social milieu of the school Parent circles
Measure at the Class Level	Class rules against bullying: clarification, praise and sanctions Regular class meetings Role playing, literature, cooperative learning Common positive class activities Class meeting teacher – parent/children

Figure 8 – cont'd
Components of Olweus' Bullying Intervention Program

Measures at the Individual	Serious talks with bullies and victims
	Serious talks with parents of involved students
	Teacher and parent use of imagination
	Help from "neutral" student
	Help and support for parents of bullies and victims
	Change of class or school

For this contest, during October's National Bullying Prevention Awareness Month, the DA enlisted students to create a 60 second video that addressed "Being Bully Free, Starts with Me" demonstrating how young people can intervene when faced with cyberbullying. The contest's submission period began October 6 and ended November 10. The students of the winning videos (first through third) were honored at a December celebration and featured on the San Francisco District Attorney's website. They also received prizes such as a gift card, Jawbone Jambox Classic and a signed baseball from the San Francisco Giants.

According to Gascón, "Cyberbullying continues to be a serious problem with nearly 70 percent of young people reporting seeing frequent bullying online. For the contest, we asked students to not only create thoughtful and innovative solutions to prevent cyberbullying, but to also consider their role in creating a bully free environment" (The Holmes Education Post, 2014).

Since bullying is an epedimic in today's society with numerous factors contributing to bullying acts, it is imperative that schools implement activities that bring attention to bullying. Researchers advocate that intervention programs on bullying will be most effective if they target mutiple environments such as the home, community and school (See Social-ecological framwork in Figure 3).

As we consistently implement these types of activities coupled with others strategically planned for the entire educational environment such as the National Bullying Prevention Month established by StompOutBullying.org and Pacer's National Bullying Prevention Center to promote the awareness and dangers of bullying, this will serve a strong means to eradicate bullying in schools.

STEP V – Reinforcement Knowledge Questions

1. How can school officials eradicate bullying through the involvement of school and community organization?

2. How can school officials address bullying on a school level?

3. How can school officials address bullying on a class or individual level?

Step VI-Communicate Impact

Bullying (whether traditional or cyber bullying) impacts the victims as well as their families. To eradicate bullying, we must understand the impact of it. We must also communicate the impact bullying has on the lives of students and the school community as a whole.

In Steps 1 – 5 of the model, we noted the need to educate stakeholders, review policies, procedures and laws, address accountability, discuss characteristics of bullying and their signs and prevent bullying through the involvement of school and community organizations. In Step VI, we communicate the impact of bullying through the documentary movie "Bully," by Lee Hirsch. We also communicate the impact of bullying through real-life stories of individual who committed suicide due to cyber bullying.

In "Bully," the public sees a compelling view of the effects of bullying. This movie depicts the tragedies of students who have been affected mentally and physically by their bullies, as well as the seriousness of the problem across ethnic, geographical and economic boundaries.

First, there is Alex, a timid 12-year old seventh grader from Sioux City, Iowa who was repeatedly threatened on the school bus, called offensive names such as "Fish Face" and punched by his perpetrators. To avoid making waves, Alex tells his concerned parents the classmates are "just messing with him." Second, there is Kelby, a 16-year old high school basketball star-athlete from Tuttle, Oklahoma. Kelby was ridiculed when she announced being a lesbian, called derogatory names such as "faggot" and faced bigotry by stakeholders at the school. Kelby was determined to remain in Tuttle despite her parents' wishes to leave the city to avoid the unnecessary and unwanted abuse by her bullies.

Third, there is Ja'Meya, a quiet 14-year old girl from Yazoo County, Mississippi who was repeatedly teased by her bullies on the school bus. Pushed to the brink, Ja'Meya took her mother's handgun on the school bus to stop her perpetrators. She was charged with multiple felony counts and placed in a juvenile detention facility. Fourth, there is the story of 17-year old Tyler from Murray County, Georgia who was overpowered by the bullying acts of classmates, indifferences of school officials and hanged himself in his parent's home. According to Tyler's father, David Long, "I knew he would be victimized at some point in time. He had a target on his back. Everybody knew that."

Finally, there is the story of Ty, an 11-year old from Perkins, Oklahoma who committed suicide as a result of bullying. His grief stricken parents, Kirk and Laura Smalley, are determined to prevent other children from been tormented from bullying and launched an anti-bullying organization called "Stand for the Silent." According to the father: "We are nobody and if it had been some politician's son, there would be a law tomorrow" (The Holmes Education Post, 2012).

If you have ever lost a loved one, particularly, a child to a tragedy, it is a feeling that can take your breath away, so to speak. Some people never get over it and others seek some level of peace by organizing civic activities to address the issue. The movie, "Bully" brings needed attention to this issue and calls for a nation to act.

Parents such as the Smalley's are calling on people across the nation to "Stand for the Silent" to end bullying and save children's lives.

This campaign encourages children to become aware of the dangers of bullying and inform authorities when they see bullying occurring.

Just as traditional bullying, cyber bullying has the same psychological and physical effect on individuals such as academic performance, stress, illness and death. It can damage an individual through social aggression such as self-esteem. It can damage an individual through relational aggression such as peer relationships. It can also damage an individual through indirect bullying such as involving a third person's email and sending an inflammatory message (Lightburn, 2009).

Because of the impact of cyber bullying, a number of individuals have committed suicide. The following provides a narrative of some real-life stories of cyber bullying in the U.S. and abroad.

Phoebe Prince was a 15-year-old student in Massachusetts who committed suicide after reportedly experiencing cyber bullying from the ongoing harassment and taunting through social networking websites and cell phone text messages by her classmates (Norman & Connolly found in Herrera, 2014).

Natasha MacBryde was a 15-year-old student of the U.K. who committed suicide after receiving online threats through a social networking website (Norman & Connolly found in Herrera, 2014).

Tyler Clementi was a 18-year-old college student who committed suicide (jumping from a bridge) as result of being a victim of cyber bullying and online humiliation regarding his sexual orientation (Schwartz found in Herrera, 2014).

Jessica Logan was 18-year-old who committed suicide (hanged herself) after experiencing cruel acts of cyber bullying. This was the result of nudes pictures of herself that she had once sexted to a former boyfriend that went viral (Schwartz found in Herrera, 2014).

Megan Meier was a 13-year-old girl who committed suicide (hanged herself) after reportedly receiving cruel MySpace messages from a former boyfriend who used a fictitious identity (Lightburn, 2009).

Ryan Patrick Halligan was a 13-year-old boy who committed suicide after being cyber-bullied. The bullying initially started in the fifth grade and infrequently through eighth grade where it intensified. The victim befriended a girl online to combat a rumor that he was gay but was humiliated when he learned his personal statement online was sent to the girl's friends (Lightburn, 2009).

David Knight was an Ontario teen who was forced to complete high school through home school due to being cyber bullied. Reportedly, schoolmates of the victim created an inflammatory webpage saying "Welcome to the Page that Makes Fun of Dave Knight," and they enlisted the social networking community to participate in the campaign. As part of the harassment, Knight was accused of being a pedophile, as well as using date rape drugs on little boys. He lost his sense of belonging with peers in the school community (Lightburn, 2009).

Ghyslain Raza was a Canadian teen who was cyber bullied when he created a film of himself emulating a Star Wars fight scene. With the film being posted on the Internet by Raza's classmates and downloaded millions of times, "the video gained global media attention and Raza was dubbed by the media as the Star Wars Kid. Raza was humiliated by the overwhelming attention. It forced him into psychiatric care" (Jackson found in Lightburn, 2009).

Sarah Lynn Butler was a seventh grade student who committed suicide as result of her being teased at school and receiving bullying messages on her MySpace page (PureSight).

Ronan Hughes was a 17-year-old boy from Northern Ireland who committed suicide after "being blackmailed into posting of himself online" (PureSight).

Grace McComas was a 15-year-old student from Baltimore who committed suicide on Easter Sunday after months of being cyber bullied (PureSight).

David Molak was a sophomore in high school who committed suicide (hanged himself) after being harassed repeatedly of cyber bullying (PureSight).

Rachel Nebiett was a 17-year-old high school student from Kentucky who committed suicide as a result of "receiving threating messages on her MySpace account" (PureSight).

Hannah Smith was a 14-year-old from England who committed suicide (hanged herself) as result of "receiving taunts on the Ask. fm social networking site" (PureSight).

Amanda Todd was a 16-year-old Canadian teen who committed suicide as a result of being bullied and cyber bullied repeatedly at different schools (PureSight).

Kenneth Weishuhu Jr. was a gay boy in his first year of high school who committed suicide as result of his being bullied online, by phone with death threats and in person by his classmates. The harassment started once he announced being gay (PureSight).

Hope Witsell was a 13-year-old girl from Florida who committed suicide as a result of cyber bullying. Reportedly, Witsell sent a nude picture of herself to a boy that she liked. The picture somehow reached its way to students at her school and other schools leading to Witsell being taunted by her peers (PureSight).

STEP VI – Reinforcement Knowledge Questions

1. From the movie "Bully," what were some of the effects of bullying?

2. From the movie "Bully," how were students bullied in person?

3. How were students bullied online by their perpetrators?

Step VII – Adopt Best Practices

Educational institutions must adopt best practices that are research-based to eradicate bullying from the school environment. Bullying leads to the victims having low self-esteem, poor grades, mental health issues, loss of friends and interest in extra-curricular activities, as well as revenge on their perpetrators.

In the resources section of this book, we highlight a number of organizations that are providing resources and intervention programs to address bullying in schools. Some of these organizations include: Anti-Bullying Alliance (http://www.anti-bullyingalliance. org.uk/); National Education Association (http://www.nea.org/ home/neabullyfree.html); The Bullying Project (http://www. thebullyproject.com/; Olweus Bullying Prevention Program (htpp:// www.violencepreventionworks.org/public/index.page), The Holmes Education Post (theholmeseducationpost.com) and Einestine Technology Services (www.einestinetechnology.com).

The Anti-Bullying Alliance is a coalition of organizations and individuals working together to stop bullying and create safe environment in which children and young people can live, grow, play and learn. The National Education Association is the nation's largest professional employee organization committed to advancing the cause of public education. NEA's 3 million members work at every level of education from pre-school to university graduate programs. The Bullying Project mission is to build a national movement to end bullying.

Since the release of Bully, the film has been screened to over a million kids, teachers, parents, and advocates. The Olweus Bullying Prevention Program is a whole-school approach model that addresses school bullying with proactive and reactive measures on the school, class and individual levels. OBPP is the most used program in the world, and it includes strategies to involve the parent and community in the whole-school approach model. The school stakeholders such as administrators, faculty and staff are responsible for the implementation of the program with the goal of improving student relations and making the educational climate safe and positive for learning (Fegenbush, 2010).

In addition to an Online National Anti-Hazing Curriculum designed to eradicate hazing and bullying from the institution's culture, The Holmes Education Post formed partnership with Einestine Technology Services and developed an Online National Anti-Cyber Bullying Curriculum to address the dangers of cyber bullying in schools. This book serves as the reference guide for the online program. Using a whole-school approach, the objectives of the online program are to educate school stakeholders (students, parents, faculty members, etc.) on the policies, procedures and laws on anti-bullying preventions and provide an understanding of the negative effects of cyber bullying. The online program includes a clear and colorful presentation; user friendly and very engaging; multiple choice questions with response explanations; test results of answer choices; passing percentage of performance; and easy to read and listen to information during the training.

The online program is also equipped with a 24-hour Web Based Reporting, Tracking, Training and Documentation System for individuals to report bullying incidents anonymously from home, school or work. The proceeding chapter provides additional information about these initiatives to support the critical needs of educational institutions.

STEP VII – Reinforcement Knowledge Questions

1. What are some organizations that are providing resources and interventions to address bullying in schools?

2. What are the objectives for the online program developed by The Holmes Education Post and Einestine Technology Services?

3. What are some features of the online program developed by The Holmes Education Post and Einestine Technology Services?

Step VIII-Teach Anti-Cyber Bullying Curriculum

Bullying is an integral part of the American culture. It occurs "when a student is exposed, repeatedly and over time to negative actions on the part of one or more students and he or she has difficulty defending himself or herself" (Olweus cited in Wood, 2013). To eradicate bullying from the school culture, we must help students recognize and understand the seriousness and dangers of it. We must help students to better understand how to cope and prevent bullying whether it occurs in the classroom, on the street or through electronic means. Just as we teach English across the curriculum, we must teach anti-bullying prevention strategies across the curriculum. The curriculum must be evidence-based to meet the needs of students in the school setting.

In fact, this model must reflect a multi-disciplined approach that provides year-long training and activities to all parties (students, parents, faculty members, etc.) about the dangers of cyber bullying. This type of whole-school approach model resembles programs such as The Holmes Education Post/Einestine Technology Services (THEP/ETS) Online National Anti-Cyber Bullying Curriculum. The whole-school approach allows schools to involve the entire constituents associated with the educational environment since bullying is a systemic problem (Smith, Schneider, Smith & Ananiadou cited in Wood, 2013).

For THEP/EST online program (See Figure 9), the training teaches students about the policies, procedures and laws on anti-bullying preventions; and provides them an understanding of the negative effects of cyber bullying. The online program is equipped with a 24-hour Web based reporting and tracking system for individuals to report bullying incidents anonymously from home, school, work and community (See Figure 10).

The training also teaches students how to deal with bullying through interventions such as peer mediation and community service projects. For teachers, the training teaches ways to incorporate activities in the lessons such as essays on bullying preventions. For parents, the training teaches them about anti-bullying preventions that are in place at the school to protect their children from dangerous acts of bullying. The training teaches parents research-based strategies on "What To Do" when their children are bullied online. For example, parents should have a conversation with their children about social media sites and incorporate rules with them regarding appropriate use of these sites. Parents should establish a Code of Conduct with their children regarding things they should not say or do on social media sites such as harassing or posting any information without a person's permission and posting their personal information online such as a telephone number and mailing address.

Additionally, parents should keep abreast of their children's conversation online, have their children ignore, block, unfriend, unfollow or untage offensive messages sent to them online. In the event that their children continue to receive inappropriate messages online, parents should keep a record of the messages with dates and time posted about their children and report information immediately to the school authority, police or Internet service provider such as Facebook and Instagram (Pacer's National Bullying Prevention Center). Parents should also keep a record of offensive messages sent to their children via cell phone and report harassment to the mobile phone provider who can take action against violators of phone policy (Curry, 2016).

THEP/ETS online program or training also teaches parents how to recognize the characteristics and signs of bullying so they can immediately get help for their children. For school administrators, the training teaches them how to evaluate the effectiveness of activities on bullying preventions in the school setting.

As a supplement to this online program, it is important that school leaders build strong relationships with their students in the educational environment so that they become compelled to inform the authorities directly or anonymously of any form of bigotry or harassment confronting their safety, health or life. Having a positive learning environment where students and teachers are socially and intellectually interacting with each other can be helpful in the implementation and investigation of anti-bullying programming (Banks, 2011).

Brochure (Figure 9)
Online National Anti-Cyber Bullying Curriculum

1. | **Curriculum Objectives**

An online curriculum using a whole-school approach to educate students and other stakeholders on:

Online National Anti-Cyber Bullying Curriculum – cont'd

- Policies, procedures and laws on anti-bullying preventions
- Psychological and physical effect of cyber bullying
- Research based strategies to address the seriousness and dangers of cyber bullying in the home, school and community

2. Curriculum Design

- 45 minute online program for students and parents in a nine module format
- 45 minute online program for faculty members in a nine module format
- 25-30 test your knowledge questions for students and faculty members
- Anti-bullying vocabulary list

3. Other Curriculum Resources Available

- An Operational Checklist for easy implementation in schools
- A customized book aligned with the online program on "Eradicating Cyber Bullying through Online Training, Reporting & Tracking System
- Access to the training through an Online Learning Management System
- Technical support team available to assist students and faculty members

4. Program Features

- Available in multiple platforms including OSX, Android and Windows
- Device agnostic (tablet, phone, laptop)

Web Based Reporting, Tracking, Training &
Documentation System (Tell24-7.com)

What?

Students can report cyber bullying incidents anonymously from home, school, work and community through the Web.

How?

Schools will be assigned an access Identification number for their students once they are registered on the Web Based Reporting and Tracking System.

What's Reported on the Reporting System?

Students can report who is the victim and bully.

Students can attach a video or picture to go along with the reporting of the incident.

Students can fully describe the incident and note the place of the occurrence.

What's obtained on the Tracking System?

The system maintains data on all students who report a cyber bullying incident.

The system maintains data on where the cyber bullying incident is occurring such as the home, school, work and community.

The system maintains data on stakeholders at the school such as students, parents and teachers who have taken the Online Anti-Cyber Bullying Training.

Web Based Reporting, Tracking & Documentation System– cont'd

What are some Benefits of the Web Based Reporting & Tracking System?

Schools can ensure that students have a mechanism to anonymously report cyber bullying incidents 24-hours a day.

Schools can concentrate on where cyber bullying incidents occur and employ appropriate resources (human and financial) as needed.

Schools can designate individuals such as a counselor, resource officer or administrator who they would like to receive the documentation regarding the bullying incident

Schools can assess the effectiveness of the system on a formative and summative basis.

An effective way to build positive relationships with students is through the Appreciative Advising framework (AA). Appreciative Advising is a research-based strategy to help schools deliver the best quality of education for students to succeed. AA's framework comprises of six phases: Disarm, Discover, Dream, Design, Deliver and Don't Settle. Disarm involves making a positive first impression with students and allaying any fear or suspicion they might have of meeting with the advisor. Discover is spent continuing to build rapport with students and learning about their strengths, skills and abilities.

Dream involves uncovering students' hopes and dreams for their future. Design co-creates a plan for helping students accomplish their dreams. Deliver is the implementation phase where students carry out their plan, and the advisor's role is to support them as they encounter roadblocks. Don't Settle involves challenging the students to achieve their full potential, according to Jennifer Bloom a former clinical professor at the University of South Carolina (The Holmes Education Post, 2015).

Another way to cultivate meaningful relations with students while fostering a positive learning environment is to utilize the training toolkit on bullying in the classroom by the U.S. Department of Education. This toolkit comprises of two modules designed to help teachers (1) identify and efficiently intervene when bullying occurs in the educational environment and (2) use effective strategies to build a classroom climate where bullying is less likely to occur in the environment.

STEP VIII – Reinforcement Knowledge Questions

1. What is the benefit of a whole-school approach to address bullying in the school?

2. What is the purpose of the Web Based Reporting, Tracking, Training and Documentation System?

3. How does the online program train school stakeholders such as students and teachers on anti-bullying preventions?

Step IX-Evaluate Strategies

Bullying is similar to a cancer. In order to end it, you have to determine the cause for the problem, provide the appropriate interventions or strategies and then monitor the effectiveness of the strategies to determine if the problem is resolved. In the first eight steps of the model, we discussed the plan for eradicating bullying from the school culture. Step IX of the model is to evaluate periodically the anti-bullying prevention strategies at the school.

While many schools use a variety of bullying prevention programs to address the dangers of bullying, there is insufficient research on the evaluation of these programs. According to research, "there is little data to support accurate data collection procedures, well validated outcome measures, and procedures to ensure consistent program implementation" (Leff, Power, Manz, Costigan, & Nabors cited in Wood, 2013).

As such, we propose concepts of the Malcolm Baldrige Model (See, Plan, Do, Check). While using this model in a previous educational setting, it required us to (1) "See" or assess what the needs are in the educational environment; (2)"Plan" appropriately the goals in line with the needs or assessment of the environment; (3) "Do" or carryout the necessary activities to meet the goals and (4) "Check" or evaluate the activities to determine if the goals were met. Figure 11 provides an illustration of this model to evaluate the nine strategies mentioned in this book to eradicate bullying from the school culture. For effectiveness, schools must establish an anti-bullying committee to work closely with the appropriate school officials. Because bullying is deeply rooted in the American culture, schools should consider hiring the necessary support staff such as an anti-bullying coordinator who reports directly to the building principal.

Figure 11

Evaluate Strategies of Model

See	Assess the school and community environments and understand the meaning of bullying from a historical, psychological and legal perspective
Plan	Educate stakeholders; review policies, procedures and laws; address accountability; discuss the characteristics and signs of bullying; implement activities; communicate impact; adopt best practices; and teach anti-bullying curriculum
Do	Incorporate the Nine Steps of the model including the 24-hour Web based reporting and tracking system for students to report bullying incidents anonymously from home, school or work; and incorporate other research-based anti-bullying prevention activities
Check	Evaluate periodically the Nine Steps of the model including the 24-hour Web based reporting and tracking system for students to report bullying incidents anonymously from home, school or work; and other research-based anti-bullying prevention activities

Figure 12 provides a summary of the nine-step model on "what to do" to eradicate bullying in the school, home, community and workplace through the resource of an Online National Anti-Cyber Bullying Curriculum and Web Based Reporting, Tracking, Training and Documentation System. The acronym, "ERADICATE" is used for better understanding and reinforcement of the strategies in the educational environment.

Figure 12

	Nine-Step Model
E	Educate students, parents and teachers on policies, procedures and laws bullying
R	Review routinely policies, procedures and laws on bullying
A	Address and ensure all students and teachers are accountable to policies, procedure and laws on bullying
D	Discuss the characteristics of the Bully, Victim, Bully-victim and Bystander; and the Signs of Bullying
I	Implement activities in educational setting on anti-bullying prevention strategies
C	Communicate the impact of bullying
A	Adopt best practices on eradicating bullying utilizing the 24-hour Web Based Reporting & Tracking System
T	Teach anti-bullying curriculum in educational setting
E	Evaluate periodically anti-bullying prevention strategies in educational setting

STEP IX – Reinforcement Knowledge Questions

1. What is an evaluation model that can be used to assess the effectiveness of THEP/ETS' Online Anti-Cyber Bullying Curriculum?

2. What are the four components of the Malcolm Baldrige Model?

3. What are components of the nine-step model to eradicate bullying from the school, home, community and work?

RESOURCES

The Holmes Education Post, an education focused Internet newspaper that provides information on improving education. The website address is: theholmeseducationpost.com. What can you find on this site?

- *Educational articles to support students, parents, teachers, school administrators, professors and college administrators*
- *Ideas and educational best practices*
- *Listing of high school, undergraduate and graduate scholarships*
- *Videotapes of classroom lectures that demonstrates teaching methods such as Whole Brain Instruction*
- *Recordings of talk shows on various educational topics*
- *Books that focus on improving education*
- *Pilot Online National Anti-Hazing Curriculum for educational institutions*
- *Pilot Online National Anti-Bullying Curriculum for public & private school systems*

Anti-Bullying Alliance – http://www.anti-bullyingalliance.org.uk/
    Mission: The Anti-bullying Alliance is a coalition of organizations and individuals working together to stop bullying and create safe environments in which children and young people can live, grow, play and learn.

BullyPolice.org – http://www.bullypolice.org/
    Mission: A watch-dog organization that advocates for bullied children and reports on State Anti Bullying Laws.

Bullying.org – http://www.bullying.org/
    Mission: Bullying.org is dedicated to increasing the awareness of bullying and to preventing, resolving and eliminating bullying in society.

Center for Parent Information and Resources (CPIR)
http://www.parentcenterhub.org/about-us/
> Mission: CPIR serves as a central resource of information and products to the community of Parent Training Information Centers and the Community Parent Resource Centers, so that they can focus their efforts on serving families of children with disabilities.

Einestine Technology Services – www. http://einestinetechnology. com/ Because of the psychological and physical effects of hazing and bullying, ETS formed a partnership with The Holmes Education Post to create both an Online National Anti-Hazing Curriculum and Online National Anti-Bullying Curriculum for schools and organizations.

CREW (http://www.va.gov/ncod/crew.asp)

CREW (Civility, Respect, and Engagement in the Workplace) offers trained facilitators to meet with employees of selected work groups at the employers' worksite for approximately six weeks. The meetings provide an opportunity for employees to engage in workgroup-level interactions about civility and their work climate. Through CREW, employees also "share positive experiences with each other and practice new behaviors that can become the cultural norm." At the meetings, facilitators engage in problem-solving initiatives and facilitate activities to enhance employee relationships in the organization. CREW was first launched by the Veteran Affairs in 2005 and has been used by more than "1,200 VA workgroups to establish a culture of respect and civility in their organization." CREW is managed by the National Center for Organization Development. Some of its outcomes include reduced sick leave usage, reduced EEO complaints, and improved employee satisfaction.

SHRM (Society for Human Resource Management (https://www. shrm.org/about-shrm/pages/default.aspx)

"The Society for Human Resource Management (SHRM) is the world's largest HR professional society, representing 285,000 members in more than 165 countries. For nearly seven decades, the Society has been the leading provider of resources serving the needs of HR professionals and advancing the practice of human resource management. SHRM has more than 575 affiliated chapters within the United States and subsidiary offices in China, India and United Arab Emirates."

Josephson Institute – https://charactercounts.org/resources/youthviolence/
   Mission: To improve the ethical quality of society by changing personal and organizational decision making and behavior.

National Association of School Psychologists –
www.nasponline.org/resources/bullying/
   Mission – National Association of School Psychologists empowers school psychologists by advancing effective practices to improve students' learning, behavior, and mental health.

National Education Association – http://www.nea.org/home/neabullyfree.html
   Mission – The National Education Association (NEA) is the nation's largest professional employee organization committed to advancing the cause of public education. NEA's 3 million members work at every level of education—from pre-school to university graduate programs.

Olweus Bullying Prevention Program (OBPP) –
http://www.violencepreventionworks.org/public/index.page
   OBPP is a whole-school program that has been proven to prevent or reduce bullying throughout a school setting with over thirty-five years of research and successful implementation all over the world.

Pacer's National Bullying Prevention Center – http://www.pacer.org/bullying/about/

> Mission: Founded in 2006, PACER's National Bullying Prevention Center actively leads social change, so that bullying is no longer considered an accepted childhood rite of passage. PACER provides innovative resources for students, parents, educators, and others, and recognizes bullying as a serious community issue that impacts education, physical and emotional health, and the safety and well-being of students.

Public Justice – http://publicjustice.net/what-we-do/anti-bullying-campaign

> When schools fail to protect children and take appropriate steps to respond to bullying, Public Justice's Anti-Bullying Campaign is designed to hold schools accountable.

Stand for the Silent – http://www.standforthesilent.org/

> Stand for the Silent was started in 2010 by a group of students from the Oklahoma State University – Oklahoma City Upward Bound Chapter after they heard the story of Kirk and Laura Smalley's son. Ty Field-Smalley. At eleven years-old, Ty took his own life after being suspended from school for retaliating against a bully that had been bullying him for over two years. Stand for the Silent exist as a platform to allow Kirk and Laura to share their story and offer education and tools that will prevent their tragedy from happening to another child and family. Kirk and Laura's mission is to continue to change kids' lives and bring awareness to bullying and the real devastation it causes.

StompOutBullying.org – http://www.stompoutbullying.org/

> Mission: StompOutBullying.org focuses on reducing and preventing bullying, sexting, cyberbullying, and other digital abuse, educating against homophobia, hatred and racism, decreasing absenteeism at school, and deterring violence online, in schools and communities across the nation.

Stopbullying.gov – http://www.stopbullying.gov/
Mission: StopBullying.gov provides information from various government agencies on what bullying is, what cyberbullying is, who is at risk, and how you can prevent and respond to bullying.

The Bully Project – http://www.thebullyproject.com/
Since the release of Bully, the film has been screened to over a million kids, teachers, parents, and advocates. The mission is to build a national movement to end bullying.

Teaching Tolerance – http://www.tolerance.org/about
Mission: Founded in 1991 by the Southern Poverty Law Center, Teaching Tolerance is dedicated to reducing prejudice, improving intergroup relations and supporting equitable school experiences for our nation's children.

REFERENCES

American Society for the Positive Care of Children. Bullying statistics and information. Retrieved May 30, 2017, from http://americanspcc.org/bullying/statistics-and-information/

About OSHA. Ocupational Safety & Health Administration. Retrieved May 15, 2016 from, https://www.osha.gov/about.html

Bame, R. M. (2013). A historical study on workplace bullying. Doctoral dissertation. Retrieved from ProQuest (15119998666).

Bank, E.J. (2011). Elementary and Middle School Bullying: A Delphi analysis of successful prevention programming. Retrieved from ProQuest (86076112)

Behavioral Management. Bullying statistics. Retrieved March 30, 2011, from Behavioral Management: http://behavior-management.com/bulling-statistics

BullyPolice.org. Programs that work. Retrieved April 2, 2015, from http://www.bullypolice.org/program.html

Bullying Statistics. Stop bullying now review. Retrieved April 2, 2015, from http://www.bullyingstatistics.org/content/stop-bullying-now-review.html

Center for Disease Control (2015). Trends in the prevalence of behaviors that contribute to violence, National YRBS 1991 – 2015. Retrieved May 30, 2017 from, https://www.cdc.gov/healthyyouth/data/yrbs/pdf/trends/ 2015_us_violence_trend_yrbs.pdf

CREW (2016). CREW: Civility, Respect, and Engagement in the Workplace.

Retrieved May 15, 2016, from https://www.foh.hhs.gov/library/ factsheets/CREW_Factsheet.pdf

Curry, L. (2016). Beating the workplace bully: A tactical guide to taking charge. New York, NY: American Management Association.

Chang, Glenna C. (2011). The hidden curriculum: Hazing and professional identify. Doctoral Dissertation. Retrieved from ProQuest (757558751).

DINatale, V. (2014, September 8). Dept. of Education launches new anti-bullying tools. Retrieved April 2, 2015 from, http:// savannahnow.com/accent/2014-09-08/bullying-breakdown-department-education-launches-new-anti-bullying-tools

Education Law Center. Retrieved March 30, 2011, from htt://www. edlawcenter.org/issues/bullying.html

Fegenbush, B. M. (2010). Comprehensive anti-bullying programs and policies: Using student perceptions to explore the relationships between school-based proactive and reactive measures and acts of bullying on Louisiana High School Campuses. Doctoral dissertation. Retrieved from ProQuest (506439312).

Herrera, J. (2014). The impact of training on faculty and student perceptions of cyber-bullying in an Urban South Central Texas Middle School. Doctoral dissertation. Retrieved from ProQuest (1697504095).

Hinduja, S. & Patchin, J.W. (2015). Cyber bullying legislation and case law. Retrieved May 30, 2017 from, htpp://cyberbullying-org/ cyberbullyinglegal-issues.pdf

Hirsch, L. (2012). The bully project. Retrieved October 28, 2013 from, http://www.thebullyproject.com/

Hodgins, M., MacCurtain, S., & Mannix-McNamara, P. (2014). *Workplace bullying and incivility: a systematic review of interventions. International Journal of Workplace Health Management.* Retrieved from ProQuest (1500629108).

Holmes, R.W. (2015). *How to eradicate bullying.* Bloomington, IN: AuthorHouse.

Holmes, R.W. (2013). *How to eradicate hazing.* Bloomington, IN: AuthorHouse.

Holmes, R.W. (2014). *Your answers to education Questions.* Bloomington, IN: AuthorHouse.

Holmes, RW. (2016). *Eradicating workplace bullying: A guide for every organization.* Bloomington, IN: AuthorHouse.

Institute on Family & Neighborhood Life. *Fact Sheet.* Retrieved April 2, 2015, fromhttp://www.spannj.org/pti/Fact_Sheet_on_Bullying_Harassment_&_Prevention.pdf

iSAFE (2012). *Cyber Bullying: Statistics and Tips.* Retrieved October 28, 2013 from,http://www.isafe.org/outreach/media/media_cyber_bullying

Kaiser Family Foundation. Retrieved May 30, 2017 from, http://www.kff.org/

Lightburn, M. (2009). *Cyber bullying: A content analysis of existing literature. Thesis.* Retrieved from ProQuest (305181121).

Lohmann, R.C. (2016). *Top five social networking sites used by teens.* Retrieved May 30, 2017 from, https://www.psychologytoday.com/blog/teen-angst/201601/top-five-social-networking-sites-used-teens

McCormac, M.E. (2015). *Preventing and responding to bullying: An elementary School's 4-year journey. Professional School Counseling. Retrieved April 2, 2015, from http://professionalschoolcounseling. org/toc/prsc/ current*

National Education Association (2010). *Retrieved April 2, 2015, from http://www.nea.org/*

National Bullying Prevention Awareness Week (2006). *Retrieved March 30, 2011 National Education Association: http://www. pacerkidsagainstbullying.org/NBPAW/parents.asp*

Occupational Safety & Health Administration (2016). *About OSHA Retrieved May 15, 2016, from https://www.osha.gov/about.html*

Oluga, S.O., Ahmad, A.B.H., Alnagrat, A.J., Oluwatosin, H.S., Sawad, M.O.A., & Muktar, N.A.B. (2014). *An overview of contemporary cyberspace activities and the challenging cyberspace crimes/ threats. International Journal of Computer Science and Information Security, 12, 62-100.*

Pacer's National Bullying Prevention Center. *Cyber bullying: What parents can do to protect their children. Retrieved May 30, 2017, from http://www.pacer.org/publications/bullypdf/BP-23.pdf*

Pastorek, S., Contacos-Sawyer, J., & Thomas, B. (2015). *Creating a no-tolerance policy for workplace bullying and harassment. Retrieved from ProQuest (1755485890).*

Pew Research Center (2015). *Teens, social media & technology overview 2015: Smartphones facilitates shift in communication landscape for teens. Retrieved May 30, 2017 from, http://www.pewinternet. org/files/ 2015/04/PI_TeensandTech_Update2015_0409151.pdf*

President Obama & the First Lady at the White House conference on bullying prevention (2011). Retrieved March 30, 2011, from The White House: http://www.whitehouse.gov/search/site/Bullying

PureSight (2017). Real life stories. Retrieved May 30, 2017 from http://puresight.com/Real-Life-Stories/real-life-stories.html

Sanders, R. (2017). Online harassment is on the rise. Americans want tech co.'s to stop it. Retrieved July 15, 2017 from http://www.timesrecordnews.com/story/tech/2017/07/12/online-harassment-rise-americans-want-tech-co-s-stop-it/469122001/

Sarkar, A. (2015). Step-by-step to stopping the cyber-bully: How organizations can help to tackle the menace. Human Resource Management International Digest,23, 31-33.

Stopbullying.gov. Key components in Anti-Bullying Laws. Retrieved April, 2, 2015, from http://www.stopbullying.gov/laws/keycomponents/ index.html

Stopbullying.gov. Risk factors. Retrieved April 2, 2015, from http://www.stop bullying.gov/at-risk/factors/index.html

Stopbullying.gov. Warning Signs. Retrieved April 2, 2015, from httpp://www. stopbullying.gov/at-risk/warning-signs/index.html

Study.com. Retrieved April 2, 2015 from http://study.com/academy/lesson/bronfenbrenners-ecological-systems-theory-of-development-definition-examples.html

TCA Regional News (Chicago) 01 Feb 2016. The workplace case for providing anti-bullying training. Retrieved from ProQuest (1761569627).

The Holmes Education Post (2014). How can school districts benefit from a zero-based budgeting model. Retrieved May 30, 2017 from, http://theholmeseducationpost.com/how-can-school-districts-benefit-from-a-zero-based-budgeting-model-2/

The Holmes Education Post (2014). What is a truancy initiative to keep students in school. Retrieved May 30, 2017 from, http://theholmeseducationpost.com/what-is-a-truancy-initiative -to-keep-students-in-school/

The Holmes Education Post (2015). What is the aim of appreciative advising? Retrieved April 2, 2015 from http://theholmeseducationpost.com/ 2015/01/what-is-the-aim-of-appreciative-advising/

The Holmes Education Post (2012). Is it time to stand for the silent? Retrieved April 2, 2015 from http://theholmeseducationpost. com/2012/05/is-it-time-to-"stand-for-the-silent"/

TopTenReview. 30 statistics about teens and social networking sites. Retrieved May 30, 2017 from, http://www.toptenreviews. com/software/articles/30-statistics-about-   teens-and-social-networking/

U.S. Department of Education (2012). Giving teachers tools to stop bullying. Free training toolkit. Retrieved April 2, 2015 from http://www.ed.gov/blog/2012/10/giving-teachers-tools-to-stop-bullying-free-training-toolkit-now available/

Wikipedia. The free Encyclopedia. Retrieved May 30, 2017, from https://en.wikipedia.org/wiki/Wikipedia

Wood, B. F. (2013). An evaluation of the implementation fidelity and outcomes of the Olweus Prevention Program in three elementary schools in Virginia. Doctoral dissertation. Retrieved from Proquest (1321501134).

AUTHOR'S BACKGROUND

Ronald Holmes is president and publisher of The Holmes Education Post, an education focused Internet newspaper. He is the author of 15 books, publishes articles on educational issues and offers unique, researched based solutions, perspectives, best practices, and resources to improve public education.

Ronald Holmes earned a PhD in Educational Leadership, a MED in Educational Administration and Supervision and a BS in Business Education from Florida A&M University. He also earned a MED in Business Education from Bowling Green State University. He is a former teacher, school administrator, and district superintendent.

Printed in the United States
By Bookmasters